Judo
R U L E S

PETER HULME

WARD LOCK

A WARD LOCK BOOK
First published in the UK 1997
by Ward Lock
Wellington House
125 Strand
LONDON
WC2R 0BB

A Cassell Imprint

Distributed in the United States
by Sterling Publishing Co., Inc.
387 Park Avenue South, New York,
NY 10016–8810

A British Library Cataloguing in Publication Data
block for this book may be obtained from the
British Library

ISBN 0 7063 7601 3

Design and computer page make up
by Penny Mills
Printed and bound in Great Britain

CONTENTS

ACKNOWLEDGEMENTS

My grateful thanks go to the following people:

British Judo Association **Board of Directors** for giving permission to use extracts from their book *Contest Rules*.

Dawn Chandler (*née* Gunby) who once again provided such clear illustrations that I saved thousands of words in descriptions.

Members of **Kendal Judo Club** and **Tony Macconnell's 'Judo 2000' Squad** who happily posed numerous times for Dawn's illustrations. It is one of the aspects of the sport of judo that top competitors are willing to spend time and effort in such mundane activities to help fellow *judoka*.

International referees **Marion Woodard** and **Ray Topple** for all their help. As with the competitors, they give their time willingly to help others in the sport.

Bob Willingham – his tremendous photographs, like Dawn's drawings, bring clarity to my words.

All my many friends in judo, particularly among the referees, whose help, comments and support have enabled me to complete my trilogy of judo books.

Domo arigato gozaimasu

(Note: In this book all references to male people may be taken to include females and vice versa.)

CONVERSION TABLE

1 millimetre (mm) = 0.03 inch
1 centimetre (cm) = 0.93 inch
1 metre (m) = 1.09 yards, 3.28 feet
1 kilometre (km) = 0.62 mile
1 gram (g) = 0.03 ounce
1 kilogram (kg) = 2.20 pounds, 0.15 stone
1 millilitre (ml) = 0.03 fluid ounce

Temperature conversion

$$°C = (°F - 32) \times 5$$

PREFACE

I went to a judo training day not long ago. Conducting the session was an international player – a World and Olympic medallist. Over 100 players and coaches took the opportunity to watch and learn the techniques which helped that player get to the top. Soon after, I also attended a refereeing course, taken by a top referee. Five people turned up, none of whom was a competitor or a trainer. The contrast between the two was staggering. Yet, on the mat, the men or women in blazers probably have more influence on how you fight a contest than anyone else, apart from yourself.

Why does the referee call '*matte*' when he does? What is he looking for in order to award a score of *yuko*? What causes him to give a *keikoku* penalty? These questions and many others should be in the thoughts of every competitor, as well as his opponent's throws and groundwork, when he plans his tactics. Sadly, very few fighters have more than a vague comprehension of the rules, let alone their interpretation. Quite often the look of puzzlement on their faces as a penalty is handed out shows just how ill prepared some players are.

The referee is not concerned as to who wins – as long as a contest ends with the correct result. Biased referees, despite claims from some people, would not last long. Quite apart from the bad reaction of spectators and fighters, a referee's peers are constantly watching him and any form of favouritism would be very quickly stamped out. At all international and BJA national events, referees are monitored all the time they are on the mat by the various refereeing commissions.

This book is not a full, word-by-word analysis of the International Judo Federation (IJF) rules. A copy of these can be obtained from the Head Office of your National Governing body. This book does, however, explain the major issues in the rules and encourages people to attend courses so they can fight *to* the rules rather than *within* them.

Thank you for reading this book. Perhaps I'll see you on the next course.

Peter Holme

1 A BRIEF HISTORY OF THE RULES

In the early days of judo, whenever contests took place, for example during the Japanese *shochugeiko* (summer practice) or *kangeiko* (winter practice), a high grade or *sensei* (teacher) was given the task of being the *shinbanin* (referee) and he would bring his own ideas as to what constituted a score. For example, although most contests were the best of three throws, holds, armlocks or strangles, the referee could, if he thought the fight was getting boring or prolonged, announce during the fight '*ippon shobu*'. This means 'one-point contest', and the next *ippon* would decide the fight whatever the state of the contest. In these individual matches it was not unheard of for there to be two or three couples fighting on the mat at the same time.

The 'red and white matches' (*kohaku shiai*) were different. Two teams lined up either side of the mat in grade order. The members of one team wore a red sash, and those of the other team a white sash. The lowest grades would fight first, and so on up through to the highest grades. Sometimes these would be as high as *sandan* (3rd Dan) or *yondan* (4th Dan). However, if one side was well ahead, quite often the *sensei* would put up high grades of the losing side against the lower grades of the winning side. This occasionally produced some surprising results. It was during these competitions that vocal encouragement of the fighters was first allowed. (Normally such cheering as '*akai*', red, and '*shiroi*', white, was strictly frowned upon. Spectators were expected to watch in absolute silence.)

At the end of the competition the winning team would enter a roped enclosure with their leader (*taisho*) to receive the championship banner, quite frequently from Dr Jigoro Kano, the founder of judo, himself.

EARLY INTERNATIONAL TOURNAMENTS

A contemporary description of a very early international judo tournament in the 1920s reported that both teams agreed a list of rules under which it was intended the competition should run. These were very simple and one is left to sympathize with the referee if he had to decide the winner in close contests.

Each contest was fought over three rounds of three minutes each. The fighters were allowed a second and three helpers between rounds and the scoring was the best of three *ippons*. The *judogi* (clothing) worn by the *judoka* (competitors) consisted of a jacket tied at the waist with a belt, a pair of tights and soft-soled shoes. There was just one score, that of *ippon*, although the referee was allowed to use his discretion in declaring a winner if the scores were drawn.

Bending back the fingers and hitting the hands or the feet in order to make an opponent let go were allowed. Necklocks, spinelocks and leglocks were not mentioned, and presumably allowed. However, hitting or kicking the 'tender parts' was specifically banned.

The sport of judo suffered a major setback with the advent of the Second World War, but by the late 1940s it had progressed sufficiently to have some rules written down. These were more to save players from possible injury than to give the sport spectator appeal.

Among these rules was the explanation that: 'Should either player wish to break off from fighting, for whatever reason – usually tightening the belt or adjusting his jacket – he should break clear of his opponent, requesting his opponent to let him if necessary. He should then drop on one knee and his opponent will adopt the same position and the timekeeper will stop the watch. The contest is renewed when the contestant who required the pause regains his feet.' The rule book added: 'The umpire will only allow this break for genuine reasons and will watch for attempts to use this rule to get out of difficulties or for a rest.'

Other rules included the following.

● A throw, lock or hold shall each count one point.

● When a contestant is in a standing position and skilfully lifts his opponent shoulder high, the umpire shall stop the throw and award him a point before the actual throw is made.

● Should one contestant go to the ground more than three times other than through the intended employment of throwing techniques, the umpire may award a penalty point against him, following a warning.

● The following actions are barred:

(a) Throwing the opponent on his head.
(b) Twisting or bending fingers, wrists, toes, jaw, head or spine.
(c) Anklelocks, leglocks, kidney squeeze, pinching, nerve pressing or blows.
(d) Pressing against the face.
(e) Pulling down the opponent for the purpose of beginning groundwork.
(f) Applying locks with a jerk.

In the case of any barred action on the part of any contestant, the umpire may stop the contest, according to his own judgement, and award an adverse decision accordingly or without regard to the score of points against the defaulter.

THE KODOKAN RULES

In 1951 the Kodokan (the headquarters of judo) in Tokyo, Japan, put down a set of rules which were translated into English and revised in 1955. These had almost doubled the number of sections. By now, two judges assisted the referee in officiating each contest.

The rules included the introduction of *waza-ari* (near technique) (see page 40). However, unless an *ippon* had been scored, the referee (note now changed from 'umpire') at the end of the fight had to call '*hantei*' (decision). The judges would then bring up the appropriate flag, and the referee would declare the contest won by saying '*yuseigachi*' (win by superiority). A declared score of *waza-ari* did not necessarily mean a player had won the fight if, in the opinion of the officials, 'he stalled throughout the match'.

There were now 21 'prohibited acts', including:

- dragging an opponent into a lying position without attempting a definite technique

- gripping the opponent's end of sleeves or bottom of trousers by inserting finger or fingers in them

- adopting a purely defensive posture in order to avoid defeat (crouching, retreating etc)

- deliberately going outside the contest area or pushing the opponent outside it meaninglessly

- anything likely to cause danger to the person of the opponent.

The final rule (Article 36) stated: `In the event of a disagreement between the original Japanese text of these rules and any translation thereof, regardless of the languages used, or any ambiguity in any such translation, the Japanese text shall prevail.' This assumed you could find someone who could read *kanji* or *katakana* (Japanese writing).

Judo rules were, and still are, frequently being amended, and soon there were an additional two scores. They did not appear on a scoreboard, but the referee and judges were expected to keep a mental note of them. *Waza-ari nichikai waza* and *kinsa* were the equivalent to a modern-day *yuko* and *koka* respectively. Unfortunately there were no written definitions of these, and the interpretation varied from referee to referee.

Each governing body has its own Refereeing Commission which controls the officials in that country. They see that the interpretation of the IJF rules are similar in whichever country a player is competing.

The IJF also have a strict examination procedure to ensure a high standard of referees throughout the world, particularly at events such as the World Championships and Olympic Games.

THE MUNICH OLYMPICS (1972)

Under the guidance of Charles Palmer, a new set of rules was written in time for the 1964 Tokyo Olympics; but judo was still, to many, a puzzle eight years later at the Munich Games. With the *waza-ari nichikai waza* and *kinsa* still not appearing on the scoreboard, it appeared to the uninitiated (and sometimes judo people as well) that a decision was made arbitrarily. Television and the International Olympic Committee (IOC) exerted pressure on the International Judo Federation (IJF – the sport's world governing body), and this resulted in the introduction of the *yuko* and *koka*. Basically, these constituted visual recognition of the two mentally scored actions, *waza-ari nichikai waza* and *kinsa*, but now everyone could see them on the scoreboard. Judges could, if they felt so inclined, raise an objection at such times as they were indicated by the referee. This produced much more uniformity in what constituted a particular score and considerably less outcry from losing players at the end of a contest.

The length of contests was also given a standard duration: 5 minutes for men, and 4 minutes for women and youth players. Previously they could have been anything from 3 to 20 minutes long, depending upon the whim of the organizers. In addition, the referees could, and did, give the fighters extra minutes, at the end of the allotted 'normal' time, if there was no score or equal scores and they could not

Top British international referee Marion Woodard officiating at the Tournoi de Paris.

decide who had won. It was not unheard of for a 10-minute contest to increase to 15 minutes and more.

Another major change in the rules following the 1972 Games was the indication of the outer edge of the contest area. Previously it had been a red tape, 7 cm wide. Many times a potential penalty was foiled by the player protesting that he hadn't seen the edge, so the International Judo Federation (IJF) introduced the 1-m wide red 'danger' area. They also introduced a stricter implementation of the penalties, which were already in the rules. Going out of the area earned an instant *keikoku* (warning), as did pushing your opponent out.

Because of this, judo tactics changed. This was epitomized in a British Open Championships' final, when Brian Jacks fooled his opponent, British team captain Peter Donnelly, into stepping out twice, for *hansoku make* (disqualification), without Jacks actually touching Donnelly.

Interpretations of the rules change as the fighting tactics change and new techniques are developed. For example, nowadays stepping out of the area is usually given a *chui* (a penalty). This is why it is important that you go along to refereeing courses in order to learn the current implications of specific actions.

The rules themselves are forever being changed, usually at IJF Congress Meetings. Most recent changes are included in this book in their respective sections. For example, since 1972 the passivity penalty (or 'roll-up', as it is colloquially known) has been introduced. Films of old All-Japan Championships reveal that it was very rare for the fights to be all-action. Indeed, it was not unusual for there to be periods of several minutes with nothing happening. Then there would be a flurry of action and the fight would end. To most non-Japanese spectators, the fight could be very boring during the inactive periods. Therefore a rule was introduced which stated that if there was no action from either or both players they would be given a warning for their 'passivity'. A second warning would give them a *shido* penalty, a third a *chui* penalty, and so on. Sadly, that didn't entirely do the trick, and nowadays the first offence earns a *shido*.

While on the subject of passivity, another new rule has been introduced. In an attempt to get players out of the red area, a paragraph in the 'prohibited acts' section states that if you are not attacking or defending and you stay in the danger area with both feet for 5 seconds or more you will get a *shido*.

The IJF Congress can also remove various rules. For example, the one which gave the referee the option of calling *ippon* when a player lifted his opponent from the floor to above shoulder height (an almost impossible task anyway) has been rescinded.

Future changes include the use of coloured *judogi*. Blue will be the official second suit colour at all international tournaments (it shows up the best on television). There are countries which allow any colour (usually pastel shades) in a bid to brighten up the sport. Some

countries also allow players to wear judo suits with mixed colours, that is the jacket in one colour and the trousers in a contrasting shade.

Another change currently being considered is the adding-up of scores. A set number of *kokas* will equal a *yuko*, and a set number of *yukos* will equal a *waza-ari*, and so on. Actually, this was advocated by the French Judo Federation way back in 1982. It was thrown out then, but the idea is making a comeback and could well be in vogue before the next Olympics.

Most of the above refers to *judoka* of any age or grade. However the British Judo Association forbids the use of armlocks (*kansetsuwaza*) and strangles (*shimewaza*) in competitions specifically for players under the age of 16 years. In tournaments for 'under 18-year-olds', only the top weights (over 50 kilograms for boys, and over 40 kilograms for girls) are allowed to use *kansetsuwaza* and *shimewaza*.

The rules and interpretations are under constant review, and it will do your club members a lot of good if one of you becomes a referee. If that is not possible, and admittedly it takes a great deal of time and commitment to become and stay a referee, particularly a good one, then try to persuade a senior experienced referee (they are human!) to visit your club on a regular basis. This way you can show him that new technique you are trying out and see whether he would recognize it, or what score he might give. You can also bombard him with your questions and thoughts on the rules of our sport. Such conversations can only improve your judo.

2 THE JUDO ARENA

CONTEST AREA

At international level a contest area measures between a minimum of 8 × 8 m and a maximum of 10 × 10 m. This is the fighting area (normally green or blue in colour) and includes the 1-m red 'danger' area. You can, of course, fight in the whole of this area, although staying in the red section for more than 5 seconds without any form of action is likely to earn you a penalty (see Chapter 10).

Surrounding the contest area is a 3-m wide 'safety' area to prevent injury if a player is thrown outside the contest area. If there is more than one contest area, then the safety area can be common to both, although it is usually then increased to 4 m. The whole of each combined contest and safety area is known as the **competition area** (see Figure 1).

The overall measurement of each competition area is normally a minimum of

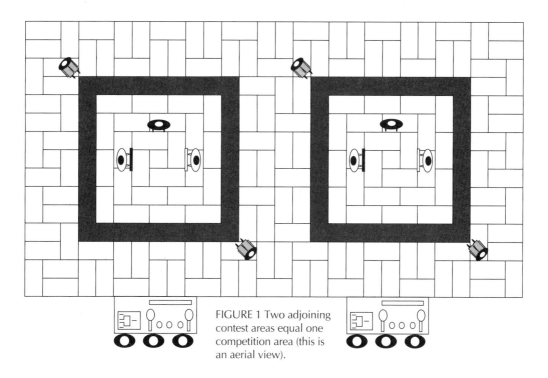

FIGURE 1 Two adjoining contest areas equal one competition area (this is an aerial view).

14 × 14 m and a maximum of 16 × 16 m. In Britain, for domestic and children's events the size can be a little smaller, although the major concern is always the size of the safety area.

MATS (*TATAMI*)

Tatami used to be made from rice straw and covered in canvas. In 1951 a specification was written, by the Kodokan, for such mats, which stipulated that they should be 3 ft (90 cm) wide by 6 ft (180 cm) long by 2½ in (63 mm) thick, and made of 'grass matting' or rice straw padding. To make a piece of padding, about 50–55 lb (23–25 kg) of rice straw was pressed to a thickness of about 2½ in (63 mm) and single stitches of hemp or linen string was woven through the material of the padding, 24 lines lengthwise and 48 stitches in a line. A number of these would be laid together, surrounded by a wooden frame and a canvas tightly stretched over the top.

Nowadays the individual mats are made, to a British Standard specification, from compressed rubber and covered in a special non-slip material. They are usually 2 m long by 1 m wide, although the latest trend is to have them as 1-m square pieces. As they usually have a non-slip base, there is rarely a requirement for a frame although occasionally they have to be pushed back together especially when the heavyweights have been fighting.

CONTROL TABLES

These are placed on one edge of the mat, facing the centre of the contest area. Placed on them, as well as the normal paperwork, are:

- a scoreboard (if it is an electronic scoreboard this will normally be on the floor to one side of the table)

- clocks or stopwatches

- flags or bats for the table officials to indicate to the referee that they have heard his calls of '*matte*', '*osaekomi*' or '*sonomama*'

- a horn, whistle, hooter or bell (or similar device) to indicate the end of a contest or the full 30 seconds for an *osaekomi* (I have also seen beanbags thrown onto the mat, towards the referee, to indicate the contest is all over)

There is also back-up equipment in case the original apparatus fails, especially when electronic scoreboards are being used.

START OF A CONTEST

The two judges are seated in diagonally opposite corners and just outside the contest area (see Figure 1) and the referee stands in the centre of the contest area, facing the control table, but a few paces back from the exact middle. On the mat are two pieces of tape, one red and one white, about 4 m apart. The red tape is always to the referee's right.

OPPOSITE A typical Control Table set up at an international tournament. The people on the front row are the scorers, timekeepers and recorders for the contest. In front of them is the scoreboard. On the top are the names of the players fighting, and underneath the scores; the letters W, Y and K stand for *waza-ari*, *yuko* and *koka* respectively. The figures directly under the name 'GAL' indicate the fighting time left in the contest. (In this picture, the referee is another top International official, Graham Turner.)

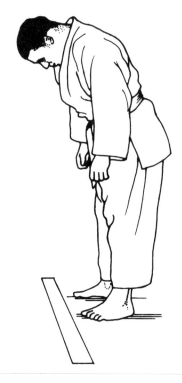

FIGURE 2 Starting bow.

The two players, one wearing the red sash/belt and the other the white, walk along the outside edge of the contest area until they are opposite these tapes. As they step onto the contest area they should bow (as though to *joseki* – where honoured guests would sit) and come to the marks, which should correspond to their belt 18colour. As they come to the marks, they bow to each other (see Figure 2), then take one further pace forward. The referee then says '*hajime*' (begin).

END OF A CONTEST

When the referee calls '*soremade*' (literally meaning 'that is all' and indicating the end of the contest) the two players go back to their starting positions, about 1 m in from their respective marks. At the same time as the referee indicates the result, the two players take a step back and bow to each other. They should then go back to the edge of the fighting area opposite the marks, bow again, and walk off along the outside edge of the contest area.

It is usual to see competitors, westerners in particular, cross the mat and shake hands after the bow. This is not strictly necessary as the bow has said it all, but is normally tolerated by most referees. However, the players should still go back to their own side of the mat and bow as they leave the contest area.

3 *JUDOGI*

The first thing you need when competing in a judo tournament is a judo suit or *judogi*. In the 1980s some players tailored their *judogi*, particularly the jacket sleeves and trouser legs. This made them difficult to grip and hold. Because of this, the regulations and measurements for these have become stricter in recent years.

COLOUR

The IJF rules currently state that your suit should be white or off-white. To distinguish between players in a contest, one wears a red tape over the top of his grade belt and the other a white tape. In Britain, players usually wear just a red or white

During the 1996 European Championships Nicola Fairbrother (Great Britain), in the blue suit, takes down Kucharzewska (Poland) in the white suit. This would not put a score on the board, but the referee and judges will have mentally scored it as a *kinsa* (see Chapter 9).

belt and leave off their grade belt.

The European Judo Union (EJU) have, for a number of years, required one player to wear a blue suit and the other a white suit in order to distinguish the players, and this is now also an option in Britain. Blue contrasts with a white suit best of all on television. This latter rule has resulted in reversible suits being the normal wear for competitors at major tournaments.

SIZE

Jacket

The jacket must be long enough to cover the hips (see Figure 3). Its recommended length can be measured by putting your arms by your sides, with your fists clenched. The bottom of the jacket should then be no higher than in line with your knuckles.

At the front, the jacket always crosses left side over right (for both men and women), and there should be a minimum overlap of 20 cm where it crosses, which should be in line with the bottom of the ribs.

With your arms extended in front of you, the sleeves should come down to less than 5 cm from your wrist joint, but they should not come any further down the arms than the wrist itself.

The gap between the sleeve and the arm should be at least 10–15 cm all the way up the arm. If you wear bandages or similar strapping on your arm, the gap is then measured from the outer wrapping of the support.

Trousers

The bottom of the trousers should lie between the ankle bone and 50 cm further up the leg. There should be 10–15 cm between the trouser and the leg itself all

the way up the leg. As with the jacket, this takes account of any bandages or supports you may be wearing.

Belt

The belt, the colour of which signifies a player's grade, is about 5 cm wide. It should be long enough to go twice round the waist, then be tied with a square knot, leaving 20–30 cm of belt hanging down either side of the knot. In Britain, the belt colours are:

FIGURE 3 Judo player (*judoka*) wearing *judogi*. On the jacket are: a GB badge on the left breast; a GB shoulder strip; a manufacturer's badge on the upper sleeve; and *judoka*'s name on the belt.

- white (beginner)
- yellow (9th *kyu*)
- orange (8th and 7th *kyu*)
- green (6th and 5th *kyu*)
- blue (4th and 3rd *kyu*)
- brown (2nd and 1st *kyu*)
- black (1st to 5th Dan)
- red and white (6th to 9th Dan)
- solid red (10th Dan).

The grades of 6th Dan and above are very rarely won in the contest arena; they are usually given for services to judo.

Men compete bare-chested under the jacket, but women must wear a plain white, short-sleeved T-shirt (not a leotard) or body top. (A leotard can prevent quick medical attention in the case of injury or illness.) The T-shirt should be long enough to be tucked inside the waistband of the trousers.

BADGES AND ADVERTISING ON JUDO SUITS

This subject has become quite an issue over the years. *Judogi* were being decorated with all sorts of additions (large badges, embroidery, different sizes and shapes of start numbers etc). Eventually, in May 1994, the IJF set down the criteria for what may be attached to a *judogi*.

Front of the jacket

On the left breast of the jacket (see Figure 3) may be sewn the highest representative badge, be it club, area or country. Its maximum size is 10 × 10 cm. On the shoulders, there may be either a sponsor's strip or the national/area/club emblem/ colours. The strip should be no more than 25 × 5 cm. On the skirt of the jacket, the contestant's name may be embroidered,

no bigger than 3 × 10 cm. On the other side of the jacket, the manufacturer's logo may appear, no larger than 5 × 5 cm.

The jacket-maker's logo, maximum 10 × 10 cm, may be placed on the upper arm of one sleeve of the jacket instead of the jacket skirt. Alternatively, it is possible to have a logo badge on each sleeve, but these must not exceed 5 × 10 cm.

Back of the jacket

The contestant's name may be embroidered in plain letters on the back of the jacket (see Figure 4). The letters, and it is recommended that there are only eight, should only be 7 cm tall. There must be at least a 25-mm gap between the lettering and the bottom of the collar, and the embroidery should not interfere with an opponent's grip.

FIGURE 4 Back of a judo jacket showing the 'start no.' panel.

17

A start number or sponsor's panel on the back of the jacket includes the Olympic abbreviation for the player's country (see Appendix A), and this should be 11 cm tall. Underneath this, the sponsor's name may appear, but it should be only 7 cm tall.

Trousers

All that is allowed on the trousers is the *judoka's* name, just by the waistband, the same size as it is allowed on the bottom of the jacket. None of the adornments should cause the wearer's opponent difficulty in holding the jacket or trousers.

Belt

A player's name may also be embroidered onto the end of the belt, again no bigger than 3×10 cm.

T-Shirt

There should be nothing printed or written on the T-shirt, which according to current regulations should be white or off-white, a neutral colour which matches the colour of the suit. If coloured suits come into vogue, then perhaps a player will be allowed to have colour-coordinated T-shirts as well.

4 OFFICIALS

In general, at any one time, there are six officials for each contest area during a competition. A referee and two judges are on the mat and three competition officials (timekeeper, scorer, recorder) sit behind a table. All have an important part to play in the running of a contest. In smaller competitions these numbers may be reduced. There could be just a referee on the mat, for example, or just a couple of people sat at the table. On the whole, however, organizers try to provide a full staff, as this means less work for the officials and fewer mistakes.

THE REFEREE

The referee is the official who moves about the mat, controlling the contest and players. He calls the scores and gives out the penalties. It is his responsibility to ensure that the fight is conducted in a safe and proper manner.

THE JUDGES

There are usually two, sitting at diagonally opposite corners, just outside the fighting area. They are there to help the referee to run the contest. They indicate when one or both of the players go out of the area. They also put forward their opinions as to scores and/or penalties if they disagree with the referee. All decisions are made on a majority-of-three basis, which explains why there are the occasional conferences in the middle of the mat.

In minor competitions, there is quite frequently just one referee, or sometimes a referee and one judge on the mat. If the latter is the case, then they consult with each other at the end of the contest, where scores are equal, before the referee announces the winner.

THE TIMEKEEPERS AND SCORERS

These operate the stopwatches and scoreboards at the calls of the referee. They should only take note of the referee (if the judges want a score or penalty changed they must go through the referee). The timekeepers have to be on their toes all the time – just one second slow in starting the stopwatches for a hold-down could mean the difference between a player being a world champion or an also-ran.

In normal circumstances, one timekeeper will time the contest and the other *osaekomi* calls. One scorer puts up the points for the red belt and the other one scores for the white belt.

THE RECORDERS

These are the officials who mark up the competition sheets and ensure that the

IJF 'A' Class referee Graham Turner (seated) indicates that, as a judge, he disagrees with the referee's *yuko* and wants a *waza-ari* score for a technique just executed.

correct competitors fight each other. Again, like the referees and other officials, they have to be very careful that no mistakes are made. As they frequently put in a ten-hour day, you can imagine the concentration and hard work required.

In international competitions outside the UK, the table officials are required to have been referees for at least three years. Britain and Northern Ireland, however, have a training scheme for table officials which accepts that they are part-and-parcel of the team and do not have to be referees first. It is a scheme much admired by other countries.

THE COMPETITION CONTROLLER AND REFEREE-IN-CHARGE

In charge of a championship is the Competition Controller (sometimes known as a Tournament Director). He organizes everything from venue to mats and medals. He is helped by a Referee-in-Charge, whose area of responsibility encompasses everything which happens on the mat. A complaint on a decision made by, or against the activities of, mat officials will be usually dealt with by the Referee-in-Charge, although he will frequently consult others, such as the Competition Controller.

5 SIGNALS

Most referee's signals are pictured throughout this book near to the relevant passage in the rules. Nevertheless, I think it would be as well to describe, all together in one chapter, the referee's and judges' signals.

REFEREEING SIGNALS

Hajime (**begin**). There are no hand signals for this. The referee stands in the centre of the mat, hands by his sides, about 2 m back from the two players, and calls '*hajime*'.

Matte (**wait**). This stops the contest and brings both players into the centre of the mat on their feet and waiting for the referee to call '*hajime*'. The referee's arm is extended straight out in front, with the palm of the hand facing forwards and fingers upwards, towards the control table (see Figure 12).

Osaekomi (**holding**). With one leg forward, bent at the knee, the arm is extended forward with palm downwards, at an angle, towards the two players. As with most signals, the referee will usually move round about 90°, while holding the signal for a few seconds, so that it can be seen by everyone (see Figure 14).

Osaekomi-toketa (**hold broken**). (The referee normally just says '*toketa*'.) As above, but the referee turns his arm with palm facing sideways and waves the arm from side to side (see Figure 15).

Sonomama (**freeze/do not move**). Except in very exceptional circumstances, this is used only in *newaza*. The referee bends forward and touches both players. He should make sure that the players do not change their respective positions while he sorts out whatever problem there may be (see Figure 11).

Yoshi (**continue**). This is very similar to the *sonomama*, except that the referee applies a little more pressure with his hands.

Ippon (**one point**). The referee raises one arm straight up above his head with the palm of his hand facing forward (see Figure 17).

Waza-ari (**near technique**). The referee puts one arm straight out to the side, parallel to the ground with the palm facing downwards (see Figure 20).

Waza-ari awasete ippon (**two near techniques equal one point**). The referee starts with the *waza-ari* signal and without pause takes the same arm into the *ippon* position.

Yuko (**effect**). The referee puts one arm

IJF 'A' Class referee Alan Rickard signalling *ippon*.

straight out from the side of his body at approximately 45°, the palm facing downwards (see Figure 21).

Koka (effect, a smaller effect than *yuko*). One arm is bent double at the elbow, palm facing forwards, fingers pointing upwards, rather like the archetypal American Indian 'How!' signal (see Figure 22).

Hantei (decision). (See Figure 5.) There are two actions for the referee. First both flags are held out in front of the body at an angle of 45°, the red flag in the right hand, the white one in the left. On calling 'hantei', he lifts the flag corresponding to the colour of the belt of the player he considers the winner, straight above his head. The judges perform similar actions at exactly the same time.

FIGURE 5 *Hantei.*

***Kachi* (victory).** To indicate the winner of a contest, the referee takes a small step forward and raises his hand, palm facing inwards, at an angle of about 45° off the vertical on the side of the winner – right hand for the red fighter, left hand for the white.

Penalty (*batsu*). The referee points to the offender with a finger as he calls the penalty. This is the same for all penalties (*shido, chui, keikoku, hansoku*) (see Figure 25). The referee will usually try to show the reason for the penalty. For example, he might take a step back with one foot to indicate a player going out of the contest area. Another reason might be fingers up the sleeve.

False attack (*semeru nise no*). Both arms, with fists clenched, are pushed straight out in front parallel with the ground, and are then pulled down to a 45° angle (see Figure 16).

Non-combativity/passivity (commonly known as a 'roll-up'). Both arms are bent at the elbows across the front of the body. The hands are rotated around each other and then a finger is pointed at the offender. If both players are given this penalty, the action is repeated for each player (see Figure 27).

No action in the red 'danger' area. While pointing with one hand to the offending fighter, the other hand is raised with palm facing forwards and the fingers spread wide (see Figure 28).

***Hikiwake* (draw).** (See Figure 6.) This is only given in team competitions. One arm is put straight above the head and, still extended, brought down in a chopping action.

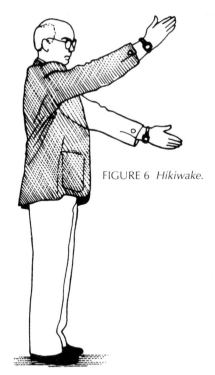

FIGURE 6 *Hikiwake.*

To indicate that a technique is not valid or not considered for a score. The referee waves one hand from side to side above the head (see Figure 7).

Cancellation (*torikeshi*) of score or penalty. To change a score or penalty, the referee waves the hand above the head while indicating the original score with the other hand. He then gives the revised score as normal.

Medical examination. Both hands, palm up, pointing towards the injured player indicate a free examination (that is one that is not recorded).

One hand, palm up, pointing towards the injured competitor allows the doctor to touch the player and tend to minor

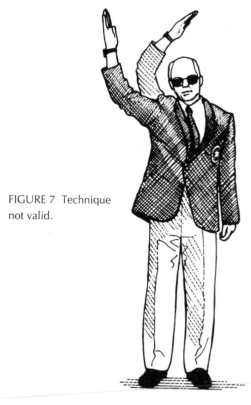

FIGURE 7 Technique not valid.

given from a sitting position. The judge will indicate a score if he has scored it differently from the referee, or he may signal the cancellation of a score, and so on. If his colleague across the mat from him agrees, they will both stand until the referee notices and changes the score to that agreed by the two judges. If the other judge agrees with the referee he either signals the same score as the referee or does nothing. Either way the score or penalty stands on the basis of the majority-of-three rule.

However, if the referee signals, for example, a *waza-ari*, and one judge wants a *koka* and the other a *yuko*, the referee should take the middle score and change his *waza-ari* to a *yuko*.

There are three extra signals in the judges' repertoire.

To indicate a technique was completed with *tori* (the player executing the technique) still in the contest area. (See Figure 8.) The judge raises his arm in the air and brings

complaints such as a nosebleed or torn fingernail, again without it being recorded.

One hand, palm up, pointing towards the injured player, with the other hand having one finger/two fingers extended, palm facing forwards, indicates whether it is the first recorded medical visit or the second (see Figure 31).

Adjust *judogi*. The referee mimes, left hand over right, tucking the jacket into the belt (see Figure 13).

JUDGES' SIGNALS

In the main, the judges' signals are the same as the referee's, except that they are

FIGURE 8 Judge indicating that a technique is in the contest area.

it down to shoulder height, parallel with the ground, and in line with the edge of the fighting area, hand vertical, and holds the signal for a few seconds.

To indicate that *tori* went out of the area before the technique was successful. As above, but the arm is waved from side to side.

Just because a judge makes one of the above two signals it doesn't mean that there has, or hasn't, been a score. All he is indicating is whether the technique was in or out. Whether it was worth a score is another decision, to be made initially by the referee and agreed to, or not, by the judges.

To show that the judge feels there is no progress in *newaza* and that the referee should call '*matte*' and get the two contestants back on their feet. With arms

FIGURE 9 Judge wanting to get players out of groundwork and back into standing judo.

bent at the elbow, the judge puts both arms out in front of him, palms upwards, and moves them up and down in a 'lifting' action (see Figure 9).

6 TIME ALLOWANCES

LENGTH OF A CONTEST

In international tournaments, the length of a contest is fixed. For both senior and under 21-year-old men it is five minutes. For women, both senior and under 19-year-old, fighting time is four minutes. In Britain, the times for younger players and the lower-graded (coloured belts) competitors is reduced, usually to three minutes.

Whatever the length of the contest decided by the organizers, this is actual fighting time. When the referee calls '*matte*' (wait), the clock is automatically stopped by the timekeeper. It is not restarted until the referee calls '*hajime*' (begin). Two other calls stop and start the watch during a fight: '*sonomama*' (freeze/do not move) and '*yoshi*' (carry on). The latter two calls are only likely to be heard when the two players are in *newaza* (groundwork).

THE END OF A CONTEST

Some players think a contest ends when the referee says '*soremade*' (that is all). However, the rules are quite clear. *The contest ends when the time allotted for the contest has expired.* So, even if there is so much noise that the bell or hooter isn't heard and something happens *after* the 5 minutes (or whatever time) have elapsed then it will not count.

Having said that, there are a couple of exceptions. First, if *osaekomi* (holding) has been called with less than 30 seconds of the time left in the fight, the contest is automatically extended until *ippon* has been scored, or '*toketa*' (hold broken) or '*matte*' (wait) is called by the referee. Second, if one of the players has started a throwing attempt as the hooter, bell or buzzer sounds, providing the result of the throw is immediately obvious then the technique will be considered for a score.

OSAEKOMI AND *TOKETA*

What constitutes a hold-down (*osaekomi*), and when a hold is broken (*toketa*), are defined in Chapter 8, but in terms of time this is what you can expect from each hold-down time segment (see Figure 10).

0–9 seconds *kinsa*
10–19 seconds inclusive *koka*
20–24 seconds inclusive *yuko*
25–29 seconds inclusive *waza-ari*
30 seconds *ippon*

The hold-down clock is started as soon as the referee calls '*osaekomi*' and is stopped when *ippon* is scored or when the referee calls '*toketa*'. When '*toketa*' is called, the timekeeper makes a note of the time, tells the referee, so that he can call the score,

Danny Kingston (Great Britain) holds Zhang (China) at the 1996 Tournoi de Paris. A few seconds after this picture was taken, Zhang submitted.

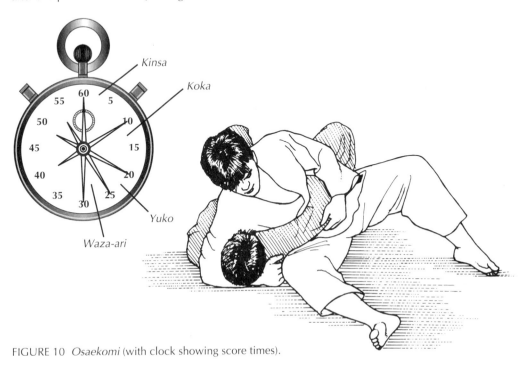

FIGURE 10 *Osaekomi* (with clock showing score times).

and then zeroes the clock. The clock is zeroed even if another hold-down is called immediately.

SONOMAMA AND YOSHI

If the players are in groundwork or actually in *osaekomi* the referee will call '*sonomama*' (freeze) if he wants to stop the contest temporarily without changing the position of the two players (see Figure 11). He may want to talk to the players, award a penalty, and so on. Calling '*matte*' may give or take away an advantage gained by a player. Having called '*sonomama*', both the hold-down clock and the contest clock are stopped until the referee calls '*yoshi*' (continue), when all clocks are started up again.

TIME BETWEEN CONTESTS

The first contests were fought in rounds, with 1-minute rests in between. When the rules changed this to a nonstop contest, players were expected to fight as and when called. A relaxation of this tradition then allowed a competitor the same length of time of rest as the duration of his next fight. Recently, this has been changed again to 10 minutes' rest between fights for international contests. In lower-standard tournaments, 'the length of the following contest' is usually the rule adopted. It is as well to check this at the start of the day if you are fighting in a competition.

FIGURE 11 *Sonomama.*

7 MATTE

The call *'matte'* (see Figure 12) is quite often incorrectly translated as 'stop'. It actually means 'wait', and is an instruction from the referee to the players to stop fighting and wait in the centre of the mat, on the mark at which they started, for him to call *'hajime'* to restart the contest.

There are nine incidents which would give the referee a reason to call *'matte'*, although the last one mentioned opens the opportunity for an almost unlimited number of reasons.

FIGURE 12
Referee signalling *matte*.

- In standing action, if any part of either player touches the mat outside the contest area. There are exceptions to this. For example if *tori* attacks with a throw such as *ouchigari* and the reaping foot goes outside the area, as long as no weight is put on the foot the referee will let the action continue. Similarly if *uke* goes outside the contest area while being thrown, providing that (1) *tori* stays in the contest area and (2) the action is continuous, the referee will allow the fight to continue until the result from *tori*'s action is obvious.

- If a player is injured or taken ill during the contest.

- When a player attempts a standing strangle (*shimewaza*) or armlock (*kansetsuwaza*) and it isn't immediately effective.

- When there is an apparent stalemate or nothing appears to be happening in *newaza* (groundwork).

- In order to apply a penalty to one or both players. (For the minor penalties, especially in *newaza*, the referee does not necessarily have to call *'matte'*).

- When a standing player lifts off the ground a player who is in *newaza* and on his back. Care should be taken by both players when the standing player puts his opponent back on the ground.

Imre Csosz (Hungary) in the blue judo suit being thrown for *ippon* by David Khakhaleishvili (Georgia) in the over 95 kilogram category of the 1996 European Championships. This picture demonstrates that a throw scores even when *uke* is outside the contest area providing *tori* stays in the area until the action is complete.

- Similarly, if a player gets to his feet with his opponent on his back, and there is a lack of control, the referee will call '*matte*', especially if the player getting to his feet lifts his hands off the mat. As with the situation described in the previous point, care should be taken as the players separate.

- When one or both players need to adjust their *judogi* (see Figure 13). If a belt or trouser cord is undone, for example, or the state of the *judogi* is giving the wearer an advantage. If the *gi* is damaged or soiled with blood, the wearer may have to leave the mat to replace it. In this case he or she should

FIGURE 13 Referee signalling to player with dishevelled *judogi*.

'*osaekomi*' has been called, he will try to put the two players back into the same situation that they were in when he called for them to break. This explains why the referee often examines the position of both players before calling '*matte*'. If he has to put them back into *newaza*, he usually calls in the judges to help him.

If '*matte*' has been correctly called, both players should come back and stand at their marks on the mat while they are adjusting their *gi* or while the referee is talking to them. The only time they are allowed to sit is if their opponent is being treated for an injury which is taking some time and the referee or corner judge indicates they can sit. If they are sitting, then for westerners it is more comfortable to sit cross-legged rather than 'Japanese style' in a kneeling position. What they should not do, and are usually stopped from doing, is wander around the mat.

be accompanied by one of the judges if of the same sex as the player. If the player is of a different sex, then another official should accompany the player to ensure that the suit is legal.

- At any other time when the referee thinks there is a need, which covers just about any situation which might arise.

Should the referee call '*matte*' by mistake in groundwork, more particularly when

8 NEWAZA

Newaza, or ground techniques, includes *osaekomiwaza* (holding techniques), *kansetsuwaza* (locking techniques) and *shimewaza* (strangle techniques).

OSAEKOMIWAZA (HOLDING TECHNIQUES)

At one time, a 'hold-down' was a very indeterminate thing. Its definition was very vague, and one version often contradicted another. However, the rules have fairly recently been changed so that a hold-down can easily be recognized. It also allows for new techniques or variations on old forms of holds to be accepted more readily.

For the referee to call and signal *osaekomi* (see Figure 14) the following must apply.

● *Tori* (the player executing the technique) must have full control of *uke* (the player receiving the technique).

FIGURE 14 Referee signalling *osaekomi*.

- To start, *uke* should have one or both shoulders on the mat. If, after the referee has called the hold, *uke* bridges, the hold-down will continue providing *tori* still has control.

- *Uke* must be largely on his back throughout the hold. If he turns onto the front of his trunk, then the referee must call '*toketa*' (hold broken) and the clock returns to zero. (This may seem an obvious statement, but I have seen a pair of shoulder blades and the front of the hips of the same young player touching the mat simultaneously.) The position of the player's back is the criterion for whether the hold is still on or not.

- It doesn't matter whether *tori* is holding from the head or the side, or on top of *uke*. As long as *uke*'s back stays largely on the mat and *tori* is controlling his opponent, he can change the hold-down position as often as he likes.

- *Uke*'s legs must not be wrapped round a portion of *tori*'s body, such as a leg (see Figure 15). Just hooking a leg will not normally be accepted as breaking the hold. *Uke* has got to show that he has full control of that leg or the trunk. If he has, then the referee will call and signal '*toketa*'.

- Hold-down scores depend on the length of time *uke* is being held (see Chapter 9).

- If a player is attempting an armlock, such as *jujigatame*, or a strangle, it is not called as a hold-down even though *uke* may be on his back and apparently under *tori*'s control. However if *tori* secures a hold and the clock is ticking and he manages to apply an armlock, such as *udegarami*, then the hold will continue. It will only stop if the 30

FIGURE 15 Referee signalling *toketa* with players in hold-broken position.

33

Morgan Ward (Midlands) strangling Daniel Harvey (Northern Home Counties) at the 1994 British Judo Association National Championships. A good example of a *shimewaza*.

seconds comes up on the clock, *uke* submits from the armlock, or *uke* escapes. The same applies with a *shimewaza*.

KANSETSUWAZA (LOCKING TECHNIQUES)

In judo, locking techniques can only be applied to the elbow joint – try it anywhere else, and you'll get a fairly hefty penalty. Although I've included them in the *newaza* section, which is where they are usually applied, they can be activated in a standing position (*tachiwaza*) as well. Be careful, however. If you are attempting a standing armlock, don't try to throw at the same time, otherwise you are likely to receive a *keikoku* penalty (see Chapter 10).

SHIMEWAZA (STRANGLING OR CHOKING TECHNIQUES)

Again, these can be applied standing or in the more usual groundwork. The same penalty as above would apply if you attempted a throw and a strangle together. The only score that can be given for either armlocks or strangles is *ippon*, that is when *uke* submits. If he doesn't tap, or escapes, then the referee may assess this as a *kinsa*, but nothing goes on the board.

TAKING AN OPPONENT INTO NEWAZA

In a judo contest, you are not allowed to drag your opponent down into *newaza* even though you may be the world's best exponent of groundwork. There are five main methods the referee will look for in a takedown (although the fifth allows flexibility for the player and new techniques to come through):

- As the result of a throw or attempted technique which doesn't score an *ippon* but knocks *uke* to the ground.

- If *tori* takes his opponent to the ground with an action which may not be a recognizable throw but is nevertheless considered skilful.

- If *tori* attempts an unsuccessful throw and falls down, then *uke* can follow him to the ground.

- If *tori* applies a standing strangle (*shimewaza*) or an armlock (*kansetsuwaza*) and, having gained some advantage from the technique, takes his opponent down, without a pause, into *newaza* (groundwork). The effectiveness of the strangle or armlock must be seen very quickly after the fighters have gone to the ground (*uke* submits or becomes unconscious) otherwise the referee will call '*matte*'. The referee will also call '*matte*' if *tori* changes the technique once having gone to ground. However, if *uke* escapes and is quite happy to continue in *newaza*, then the referee will not interfere and will let the fight carry on.

- Finally, anything not covered by the above which the referee doesn't assess as a deliberate pull-down.

In all cases, the movement from standing to groundwork must be smooth, fluid and continuous. You cannot knock your opponent down, and then wait for a couple of seconds while you decide what should follow before diving down on top of him.

If *tori* does drag his opponent down to earth and the referee decides to give a penalty, but *uke* is quite happy on the ground and turns it to his advantage, then the referee doesn't have to call '*matte*'. He can give a small penalty, such as a *shido*, without even stopping the contest. A *chui* or stronger may necessitate him calling '*sonomama*' (do not move), stopping the action so that he can give the penalty.

FIGURE 16 Referee signalling illegal pull-down and 'negative judo'.

If there is no obvious advantage being taken by the non-offender, or the person pulling down is on top, then the referee will call '*matte*' and make the signal shown in Figure 16. This means *tori* loses his advantage *and* is penalized.

9 SCORES

There are five scores for a referee to consider during a contest. One – *ippon* – ends the contest immediately. Three appear on a scoreboard – *waza-ari*, *yuko* and *koka*. The other – *kinsa* – is only mentally counted by the referee and judges.

It is common usage to translate these scores into a points value, but this is inaccurate. A player should think of scores in terms of the Japanese terminology and understand that no amount of *kokas* equal a *yuko*; any number of *yukos* can be beaten by a *waza-ari*, which in turn will be beaten by an *ippon*. The one exception is when two *waza-ari* scores are made by one player in a contest. These equal one *ippon* and thus end the fight. The term used in this instance is '*waza-ari awasete ippon*'.

FIGURE 17 Referee signalling *ippon* throw. Player throwing with *yama-arashi*.

The only occasions on which 'points' are awarded for wins are during team competitions or in a 'round-robin' type of event. In judo, the latter is referred to as the 'pool system'.

For the record, *koka* and *yuko* translate as 'effect' with a *yuko* obviously a bigger effect than a *koka*. *Waza-ari* means 'near technique' and *ippon* equals 'one point'. '*Waza-ari awasete ippon*' translates as 'near techniques together make one point'.

Scores can be obtained through either *tachiwaza* (standing techniques) or *newaza* (ground techniques), or a combination of the two. It is very difficult to illustrate throwing techniques to equate with the relevant scores. The examples I have shown are just that – examples. There are many variations. It would take a book many times the thickness of this one to cover anywhere near all of the situations which would elicit a particular score. Talking to a referee will help you recognize all the other instances.

IPPON

Ippon ('one point') can be awarded as follows.

From a throw (*nagewaza*)

See Figure 17. There are three components required for a throwing technique to be given the score of *ippon*. *Tori* (the thrower), with control, throws his opponent so that he:

- lands largely on his back with
- considerable force and
- speed.

In order to stop attempts at what is a dangerous form of 'defence', if *uke* attempts to avoid being thrown on his back by landing in a bridge (i.e. with only his head or back of neck and heels touching the mat), as in Figure 18, the referee will score the throw as though he had landed in the position for *ippon*.

From a hold (*osaekomiwaza*)

See Figure 14. The three components required for a holding technique to be given the score of *ippon* are as follows.

- *Uke* (the player being held) must be controlled by his opponent. This can be from the side, from the head and shoulders or from on top. *Tori* (the

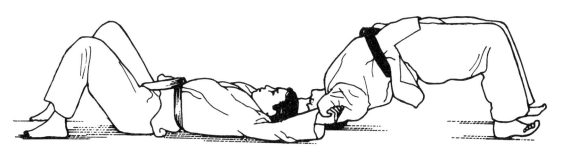

FIGURE 18 Player landing in bridging position from *tomoenage* (circle throw).

Okada (Japan) throwing Lascau (Germany) for *ippon* at the 1995 World Masters in Munich. This photo sequence, by Bob Willingham, superbly demonstrates the full requirements for *ippon* – speed, force and making the opponent land largely on his back.

player applying the hold) can change the hold as often as he wants, as long as

- *uke* is largely on his back which is in contact with the mat for a period of 30 seconds

- *Uke* should not have his legs wrapped round *tori*'s leg or legs or body or the hold will be considered as broken; the referee will call and signal '*toketa*' (see Figure 15) and the clock reset to zero.

From a strangle (*shimewaza*)

See Figure 19. *Ippon* will be given when:

- *uke* submits by tapping twice with a hand or foot

- *uke* calls '*maitta*' (which translates as 'I submit')

- *uke* becomes unconscious or when the effect of the strangle is sufficiently apparent.

FIGURE 19 Player submitting from *shimewaza* (strangle).

Frequently, players who become unconscious do not realize that this has occurred. Often they will deny they were 'out'. Great care must, and usually is, taken in this situation. In Britain, if a player loses consciousness for any reason, other than a strangle, he will be withdrawn from the competition and should not compete or practise for a couple of weeks. Following the effects of a strangle, a player must be cleared by a medical examination from someone who knows about the effects of *shimewaza*. For adults, if the unconscious state is as a result of a strangle, this clearance can happen on the same day. For juniors, the player is not allowed to continue that day, whatever the cause.

From an armlock (*kansetsuwaza*)

Ippon will be awarded when:

- *uke* submits by tapping twice with a hand or foot as a result of *tori* applying pressure to *uke*'s elbow joint

- *uke* calls '*maitta*' ('I submit').

Kansetsuwaza translates as 'locking techniques' but the elbow is the *only* joint on which you are allowed to apply the pressure. Locking any other joint will get you a penalty.

From a penalty (*hansoku make* – loss by disqualification)

Ippon will be awarded when a player is given the penalty of *hansoku make* or accumulates penalties up to *hansoku make*. This is automatically carried across to his opponent as an *ippon* win.

WAZA-ARI ('NEAR TECHNIQUE')

See Figure 20. This is called in the following situations.

From a throw

If one of the elements needed for an *ippon* is missing, although *uke* should land partially on his back, i.e. if he lands on his side, however fast and forceful the throw might be, it is only likely to score *yuko*.

From a hold

As for an *ippon*, but *uke* is held for between 25 and 29 seconds. It will be obvious that you can only score *ippon* or nothing from a strangle or armlock.

From a penalty (*keikoku* – 'warning')

When a player is given or accumulates a penalty of *keikoku* (see pages 47–48). This automatically gives your opponent a *waza-ari*. If he has already scored a *waza-ari* from a technique, he then wins the contest. This is similar to *waza-ari awasete ippon*, but in this case the term used is '*sogogachi*' (compound win).

YUKO ('EFFECT')

The referee will award a score of *yuko* to a player in the following situations.

FIGURE 20 Referee signalling *waza-ari*.

FIGURE 21 Referee signalling *yuko*. Player throwing with *okuriashiharai* (sliding sweeping ankle throw) and *uke* landing on his side.

From a throw

See Figure 21. When two of the elements required for an *ippon* are missing. It is usually scored when *uke* lands on his side, but if he lands on his back without any speed or force then the referee is likely to score *yuko*.

From a hold

As for *ippon*, but *uke* escapes between 20 and 24 seconds.

From a penalty (*chui* – 'attention')

When a player is given or accumulates the penalty of *chui* (see pages 48–50). This automatically gives your opponent a *yuko* score.

KOKA ('EFFECT' – SMALLER THAN YUKO)

A score of *koka* is awarded in the following situations.

FIGURE 22 Referee signalling *koka*. Player throwing with *ouchigari*.

From a throw

See Figure 22. When *uke* lands on his backside or thighs.

From a hold

As for *ippon* but only for between 10 and 19 seconds.

From a penalty (*shido* – 'guidance')

When a player is given a *shido* penalty (see pages 50–53). This automatically gives your opponent a *koka* score.

KINSA (NO DIRECT TRANSLATION)

This is not a score which the referee calls, but he and the judges score it mentally in the following situations.

From a throw

See Figure 23. Where a throw cannot be scored as a *koka*, but nevertheless takes *uke* to the ground, in a landing position on hands and knees, or on the front of the body. For any score to be considered, it must be as a direct result of *tori*'s actions.

From a hold

As for *ippon*, but only up to 9 seconds.

From an attempted strangle or an armlock

If *uke* escapes fairly quickly from the attempt, but nevertheless there has been an attempt.

AN ATTACK

At this level, we are talking about a very small outcome from *tori*'s efforts. As such, an attack is difficult to describe. Indeed, a high-ranking international refereeing colleague has been trying for a number of years to write a technical definition of what constitutes an attack. The following is an attempt to describe it as simply as possible.

From *nagewaza* (throwing techniques)

An attack can be broken down into four elements:

- preparation – setting the opponent up for the technique
- breaking his balance – in *nagewaza* particularly
- getting in the appropriate throwing position
- *uke* making a defensive reaction in order to avoid being thrown.

From *newaza* (ground techniques)

An attack causes *uke* to defend himself against an attempted turn-over, armlock or strangle. Judgement is based on what *tori* achieves. Attacks have to be genuine attempts at a technique, and not just a player looking busy. That is likely to get the player 'passivity' or 'negative judo' penalties at least (see Chapter 10).

FIGURE 23 *Kinsa.*

In order to decide who is the winner, the referee and judges have to take all the above points into consideration. If there is a majority score for one player or another, then the result is obvious. When the scores are equal, the referee has to use *kinsa*, attacks, or, if all else is equal, attitude to decide who wins. Then it becomes very subjective. The obvious advice is to get more scores on the board than your opponent; then the result can be in no doubt!

WHO CALLS THE SCORE?

The referee calls the scores, but the judges can overrule him. If a judge considers that the call made by the man in the middle was wrong, he signals the score/penalty he believes should be given; if the other judge agrees, he will also give the same signal.

The referee should then change the score to whatever the judges have signalled. This is known as the 'majority-of-three rule'. If the referee calls (for example) a *waza-ari*, one judge calls a *koka* and the other a *yuko*, then the referee should change his score to the middle one, in this case a *yuko*.

The only person who is allowed to change a score is the referee. If the judges want the score changed they *must* go through the referee, and not just advise the scorekeeper to change it.

THE SCOREBOARD

Figure 24 shows a typical manual scoreboard during what appears to be a very exciting contest. Electronic scoreboards are very similar, except that they usually have a contest timing clock and some form of visual countdown for *osaekomi* as well. As

FIGURE 24 Scoreboard.

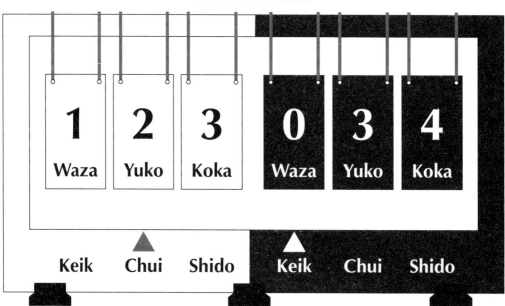

can be seen from the example, it is split in half. The drawing shows the scoreboard from the referee's side; the coloured (red, usually) side is on his right. If you have never watched a judo contest before, notwithstanding the technical explanations below, you can easily see who is winning. Think of the *waza-ari* scores as 100s, *yukos* as 10s and *kokas* as single units. If the contest shown on the scoreboard in Figure 24 were to end right now, white belt has won by *waza-ari*. All the other scores are irrelevant.

The triangles on the bottom part of the board indicate that both players have received penalties at some stage during the fight. These will have automatically added the equivalent score to the other side at the time they were given. It can be seen, therefore that white's *waza-ari* is as a result of a *keikoku* penalty given to red (see Chapter 10). White's *chui* is one of red's three *yukos*.

If red is given another penalty, even a *shido*, then he will be disqualified. The next penalty up from *keikoku* is *hansoku make* (loss by disqualification). If white scores a *waza-ari*, then the fight is also over. This time white will have won *sogogachi* (compound win).

Up to now, it has all been in white's favour. However, should he get another penalty then everything would change. In that instance, red would lose a *yuko* but gain a *waza-ari* (the *yuko* given for the *chui*

penalty will be taken off and replaced by the score equivalent to the *keikoku*). Again, if the contest ends at that point, red will have won by a majority of *koka* scores. If red scores a *waza-ari* before the end of the fight and white does nothing else, then red will have won by a majority of *yukos*, more commonly called a *yuko* win, the two *waza-ari* scores cancelling each other out.

SCORING IN TEAM EVENTS

In a team event the *ippon*, *hansoku gachi*, (win by disqualification of opponent) or *sogogachi* will give that team one contest win and ten points. A *waza-ari* win would give one contest win and seven points. A majority of *yukos* (and it doesn't matter how many of them there are) equals one contest win and five points. A *koka* win gets three points. In a team event equal scores count as a draw, and neither side gets any points. This really is the only time in judo tournaments that points are attached to wins. However, when adding up the team scores at the end of the match contest, wins are counted first. Two 'koka' wins' will beat one 'ippon' win'. It is only when the teams are equal on wins that the points come into the reckoning. If the points are equal as well, the drawn contest(s) are refought with a *hantei* at the end of each contest, if necessary.

10 PROHIBITED ACTS AND PENALTIES

At the start of competitive judo the rules were very simple. There were few restrictions on what could, or could not, be done. The additions to the rules on penalized actions, through the years, have mainly been for two reasons. Either the action was considered dangerous, or it was too defensive or slow. The emphasis on discouraging excessive defence or inactivity has mainly been due to the influence of television. At the 1996 Atlanta Olympic Games, there were more penalties for passivity given out than for any other 'illegal' action.

Penalties are divided into four groups, depending upon their severity. For a long time, penalties were not added to the score but used as a guide for the referee. Then they were included, but only put on the scoreboard at the end of a contest. Nowadays each penalty, when awarded,

FIGURE 25 Referee penalizing player.

automatically gives the other side the equivalent score at the time the penalty is handed out (see Figure 25).

Each offence is listed below in the order of penalties from the heaviest (*hansoku* – disqualification) to the lightest (*shido* – guidance). These are the normal penalties awarded. The referee can, however, if he thinks it is justified, give a heavier penalty than the one recommended.

Although punishments for illegal acts are not cumulative, once you have a certain penalty and do something which warrants another of the same, the referee must give you the next one up. For example, a player is given a *shido* penalty, then commits another *shido* offence. As he cannot have two *shidos*, he will receive a *chui* penalty. A *shido* given when there is already a *keikoku* on the board is *hansoku* (disqualification). However, if a *shido* has been given and a *chui* offence is committed, then it is only a *chui* which goes up on the scoreboard (and a *yuko* to the other side).

Each time there is a change in the penalties then the score given for the previous offence is removed from the scoreboard as the new score is added.

HANSOKU MAKE (LOSS BY DISQUALIFICATION)

This gives your opponent an *ippon*. The actions this penalty is given for are as follows.

Wearing a hard/metallic object

This can range from a metal leg calliper (this happened once at a British Open Championships) to a thin gold neck chain (this induced another disqualification at a British Open which, in turn, lost the player an Olympic place). This rule would also include:

- a hair band which has a metal piece holding it together
- a ring (and you are not allowed just to put a covering, such as a strip of plaster, over it)
- earrings, even the 'sleepers' put in newly pierced ears
- a watch or bracelet – it is amazing how many players forget they wear a watch
- a hard shin-guard, even if it is made out of plastic.

Intentionally falling backwards with your opponent on your back

This is an obviously dangerous action, particularly among the heavier competitors.

A 'head dive' while attempting a technique such as *uchimata*

This was a successful attempt to dissuade players from a dangerous throwing style which became the vogue for a little while. It caused a number of paralysing injuries throughout the world. This doesn't have to be *uchimata*. It can be any of the throws in which the head goes forward and down, such as *haraigoshi* or *yama-arashi*. Neither does the head have to come in contact with the mat. If you put yourself in the position where the head, or even worse the back of the neck, *could* hit the mat, then you will be out of the contest.

KEIKOKU (WARNING)

This gives your opponent a *waza-ari*, and is given for the following actions.

Disregarding the referee's instructions

Calling your opponent names or making rude and derogatory gestures during a contest

Both of the above are straightforward – maintaining a strong self-discipline will keep you out of any trouble of this kind.

Doing anything which might injure your opponent

Most of the rest of the *keikoku* penalties are for actions which may injure your opponent. This one is a catch-all for anything else which might come up in a contest. It includes throws such as *kanibasami* (scissors throw).

Attempting to do anything outside the contest area

If a technique is started inside the area and goes outside, it does not come under this rule unless *tori* tries something different after going out.

Doing anything which is against the spirit of judo

This covers virtually anything not written down in the rules.

Applying *kansetsuwaza* (locking techniques) to anywhere other than the elbow

Deliberately falling to the ground while applying *wakigatame* (reverse armlock)

The above two rules apply to armlocks. Indeed, throwing anyone while applying a standing armlock will get you a *keikoku*.

Applying a spinelock or necklock or any other action which might injure the spinal vertebrae

Quite often, when a player is on his stomach, his opponent, astride his back, will grab the neck and try to apply a strangle. There is a strong risk that a spine- or necklock will be applied. I have already described a situation in Chapter 7 where the referee will call '*matte*' when a player lifts his opponent, who has been lying on his back, off the ground. When he does, the player must be put gently back down on the mat. If he drops him or drives him back hard into the mat, the opponent could land on the back of his neck and sustain a serious injury. Therefore, such an action earns *keikoku* for *tori*.

Sweeping your opponent's supporting leg while he is attempting a technique such as *haraigoshi*

This is likely to drive your opponent face first into the mat, which is dangerous, and may also cause injury to his knee.

Applying *kawazugake* and falling backwards on top of your opponent

This entails entwining your leg around your opponent's leg. When you fall backwards, you will cause very serious injury to his knee. Luckily, it is not a common occurrence.

CHUI (ATTENTION)

This gives your opponent a *yuko*, and is given for the following actions.

Going outside the contest area, except as a result of your opponent's actions

If a player attacks inside the contest area and both players go out, the referee will call '*matte*' and no penalty. However, if *tori* goes out first, not as a result of *uke*'s

Ryan Birch (Great Britain) armlocking his opponent with *jujigatame* (straight armlock) at the 1996 European Championships. The pressure is only being applied to the elbow – anywhere else and the player would be penalized. The white-suited player's hand is coming up to tap his submission.

defence, then he is likely to get a *chui*. This applies particularly to an attempt at *sutemiwaza* when more than half of *tori*'s body goes outside the area (see Figure 26).

Forcing or pushing your opponent to make him go outside the contest area

If you attempt a technique at the edge of the contest area and you go out, this rule doesn't apply.

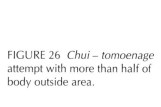

FIGURE 26 *Chui – tomoenage* attempt with more than half of body outside area.

Pulling your opponent down into *newaza*

The exceptions to this have been described in Chapter 8.

Making your opponent let go by bending back the fingers or kicking the hand with the foot or the knee

You can put your foot against the hand and push in a steady, continuous movement, but you must not kick.

Applying the action of *dojime* (leg scissors) around the trunk or neck of your opponent

There is a common misconception that you cannot cross your legs around your opponent's body. This is not quite true. What you are not allowed to do is squeeze by straightening the legs, which applies pressure to the ribcage, kidneys or the neck, which can cause serious injury.

Attempting to strangle your opponent using the belt

Using the bottom of the jacket for a *shimewaza* is also not allowed.

SHIDO (GUIDANCE)

This gives your opponent a *koka*. As this is the smallest penalty, it is the one most likely to be awarded, for offences such as the following.

Avoiding taking hold of your opponent and/or stopping your opponent taking hold in order to prevent any action in the fight

Known as *kumikata* (gripping), this is normally tolerated for a few seconds, particularly at the start of a fight, but not for much longer.

Failing to attack after you have got a hold

Having taken a hold, you are allowed approximately 25 seconds to make an attack. If you don't, the referee will twirl his hands around each other (see Figure 27), colloquially known as a 'roll-up', and you will get a *shido*. It is interesting to note that at international events (and this will quickly filter down to domestic competition) the referees have recently become much keener on giving passivity penalties. There are no passivity penalties for *newaza*. However, the referee is likely to call '*matte*' fairly quickly if there is no progress.

FIGURE 27 Referee giving passivity signal.

Not attacking or defending when both feet are fully in the red danger area for 5 seconds or more

The referee will put his hand up with fingers and thumb spread (see Figure 28) along with the pointing penalty finger.

The pertinent point here is that both feet have to be in the red area and the player has to be neither attacking nor defending.

FIGURE 28 Referee signalling that a player has spent 5 seconds in the red 'danger' area without any activity.

Giving the impression of attempting an attack when there is no intention actually to throw your opponent

This is known as a 'false attack'. The most common occurrence is drop-kneed *seoinage*. The refereeing signal for that can be seen in Figure 16 and is the same as for an illegal take-down into *newaza*.

Standing with your fingers continually interlocked with your opponent's to prevent any action

This is not really a common sight, but the time limit is around 5 seconds before the penalty is handed out.

Standing in a *jigotai* (excessively defensive) position

This also has a 5-second time limit. It commonly occurs when a player is bent at right angles from the waist, but a stiff arm preventing an opponent getting close can equally be described as *jigotai*.

Continually holding the same side of the jacket with both hands without attacking

It doesn't matter whether it is the sleeve, collar or one of each. The time limit is again 5 seconds. If your opponent ducks his head under your arm, then you can stay like that for as long as you like without penalty, providing you do not adjust the grip.

Continually ducking your head under your opponent's arm

You can possibly get away with a couple of successive ducking actions, but no more. If you do more, it will probably be looked upon as a defensive attitude and penalized as such.

Continually holding your opponent's belt or bottom of the jacket without attempting an attack

As with all the others, after 5 seconds you are likely to be on the receiving end of a *shido*.

Tying or untying your belt or the cord which holds up your trousers, or generally rearranging your *judogi* without first getting the referee's permission

Under normal conditions, the referee will stop the contest to allow you to retie your belt or trousers if you bring it to his notice. However, he will not necessarily stop the contest to let you tidy up your *judogi* if he believes no disadvantage is coming from it or that by so doing he will interrupt the flow of the fight.

Completely encircling a limb with the belt or the bottom of the jacket

Using the belt or jacket to trap the limb is perfectly legitimate, providing it doesn't go right round.

Screwing up the bottom of your opponent's sleeves or putting your fingers up the inside of your opponent's sleeves or trouser legs

You can put your fingers up your *own* sleeves (see Figure 29).

Continually and defensively holding the end of your opponent's sleeves

You can hold the end of the sleeves as

long as you are attempting a throw (for example *sodetsurikomigoshi*). No throwing attempt after 5 seconds will produce a penalty (see Figure 29).

Taking a *judogi* in the mouth

I'm not sure what advantage can be gained from this activity, but it is mentioned in the rules so must occasionally occur.

Putting your foot in your opponent's collar or belt in order to break his grip

The collar includes what would probably be thought of as the 'lapel' of the jacket.

Putting a hand, arm, leg or foot across your opponent's face

The limits of the face are defined as the

FIGURE 29   Screwing up sleeves.

normal hairline at the forehead, a line down the side of the face by the ears, and the jawline.

Taking an opponent's leg or legs with your hand or hands (unless you simultaneously put in an attack)

The emphasis is placed on the word 'simultaneous'. This also includes grabbing the trousers.

The tying of long hair during a contest will be allowed only twice. Any further stoppage of time for this purpose will be given a *shido* penalty.

In judo long hair (whether male or female) has to be tied back, usually into a pony tail, with some form of non-metallic (see page 47) fastening. A rubber band is often used but a ribbon tied in a bow is *not* allowed. Whatever is used, it frequently comes loose and the contest has to stop while it is tied again. This time is also often used by players to give themselves a short rest. The IJF introduced this rule to stop what they consider time-wasting. If you have to tie your hair a fourth time you will be given a *chui*.

The referee will generally give the *shido*, *chui* and, quite often, the *keikoku* penalties without consulting the judges. Of course the judges can overrule his decisions. However, when it comes to *hansoku*, the referee must consult the judges, if only briefly, before pointing the accusing finger.

PROTESTS AGAINST DECISIONS

Bearing in mind that, at major competitions, all decisions on the mat are on the basis of the majority-of-three officials (referee and two judges), then in general you should accept the decision. However, if you feel you absolutely must protest, there is a correct way of going about it. Sitting down in the middle of the mat and refusing to move is not going to get you any sympathy, least of all from the next two players waiting to fight.

In fact, it depends on the officials, not the players. Once all three officials have left the competition area, then it is impossible for a decision to be changed. While any one of the three is still on the mat, however, it is possible for a decision to be reconsidered. If you feel you have a legitimate objection to the result you can, politely, ask the referee/judge(s) to stay on the mat while you request the Referee-In-Charge at the tournament to come to your mat side and discuss the incident. Following that discussion, whatever decision is agreed stands. In case you feel that this will be a waste of time, I can assure you it is not unheard of for a decision to be overturned. It even happened once at an Olympic Games. It should be said, however, that spurious complaints will be given short shrift, and you will soon get the reputation of a whinger if you persistently complain for no good reason. This could spoil your chances, too, when you have a legitimate case.

11 COMPETITION RULES

WEIGHING-IN

The first hurdle to overcome at a competition is the weigh-in. Most competitors refer to their weight as, for example, *under* 71 kilograms, or whatever category they belong to. In fact, for each category (except the lowest weight group) there is a minimum weight as well as a maximum weight. If a player does not make the minimum, he is not allowed to compete, just the same as if he is over the maximum.

The senior and youth international weight categories are the same throughout the world. However, for competitions involving only players who are under 18 years old, particularly at British national level, players are subdivided into age bands as well as weights (see Figure 30).

At most international competitions, a player is allowed only one weighing on the 'official' scales. Usually, however, there are test scales available, which can be used to make sure that a player is within the limits.

In most British competitions there is no such restriction. Players can make as many attempts as they like, within the time limit allowed for weighing-in.

FIRST FIGHT

Having successfully weighed in, it is always advisable to check what time you are likely to start fighting. Remember that the time you are given is always likely to be approximate. It is best to arrive at the arena at least 30 to 45 minutes before your weight category is due on, as the previous category could finish early. (One very experienced player once turned up dead on the time given for his category at a British Open Championships, only to discover that the players in the previous weight category had been throwing *ippons* galore, and finished half an hour ahead of time. He had missed his first fight.)

The rule is quite simple, if a little strict. If you don't turn up for a contest, no matter at what stage of the competition it may be, then it will be as though you have never taken part. If you are in first-round pools and have enough wins/points before the start of your last contest in your pool, you still have to fight. Quite apart from the fact that it is better to go through as number one than number two, if you don't fight you won't go through to the next round at all.

Similarly, in a knockout competition, a non-appearance puts you out of the repêchage (the competition for first-round losers) as well as the knockout itself.

The competitors due to fight are usually called as soon as the previous fighters have started their contest. If either one or both of the players fails to show, they are given a second call after one minute. If a player

MEN & BOYS

Seniors Over 16 yrs	Juniors 18–20 yrs	Juniors 17/16 yrs	Juniors 15/14 yrs	Juniors 13/12 yrs
				+27kg to 30kg
				+30kg to 34kg
			Under 38kg	+34kg to 38kg
			+38kg to 42kg	+38kg to 42kg
			+42kg to 46kg	+42kg to 46kg
		Under 50kg	+46kg to 50kg	+46kg to 50kg
		+50kg to 55kg	+50kg to 55kg	+50kg to 55kg
Under 60kg	Under 60kg	+55kg to 60kg	+55kg to 60kg	Over 55kg
+60kg to 65kg	+60kg to 65kg	+60kg to 65kg	+60kg to 65kg	
+65kg to 71kg	+65kg to 71kg	+65kg to 71kg	+65kg to 71kg	
+71kg to 78kg	+71kg to 78kg	+71kg to 78kg	Over 71kg	
+78kg to 86kg	+78kg to 86kg	Over 78kg		
+86kg to 95kg	+86kg to 95kg			
Over 95kg	Over 95kg			

WOMEN & GIRLS

Seniors over 16 yrs	Juniors 16–18 yrs	Juniors 15/14 yrs	Juniors 13/12 yrs
			+25kg to 28kg
			+28kg to 32kg
		Under 36kg	+32kg to 36kg
		+36kg to 40kg	+36kg to 40kg
		+40kg to 44kg	+40kg to 44kg
Under 48kg	Under 48kg	+44kg to 48kg	+44kg to 48kg
+48kg to 52kg	+48kg to 52kg	+48kg to 52kg	+48kg to 52kg
+52kg to 56kg	+52kg to 56kg	+52kg to 56kg	Over 52kg
+56kg to 61kg	+56kg to 61kg	+56kg to 61kg	
+61kg to 66kg	+61kg to 66kg	Over 61kg	
+66kg to 72kg	+66kg to 72kg		
Over 72kg	Over 72kg		

FIGURE 30 Chart showing age/weight categories.

still does not appear, a third and final call is made. Should either not turn up a further minute after this last call, then the referee will award the contest to the player who *has* shown, by calling '*fusengachi*' (win by non-appearance of opponent).

REST PERIOD

In international competitions, all competitors are allowed at least 10 minutes' rest between contests. In the early rounds, of course, you will get at least this amount of time as the other players go through their fights. However, as the category proceeds through to the later stages, there are fewer contests, and if a quick *ippon* is scored there could well have to be a break in the proceedings to allow the full 10 minutes.

The rest period used to be the same length of time as the duration of your next contest, and in most domestic competitions this rule will probably still be invoked. It is always best to check with the Competition Controller as to which rule he is recognizing.

INJURIES DURING A CONTEST

If an injury occurs during a contest, the referee has to consider the following three possibilities:

- was the injury caused by the injured competitor?
- was the injury caused by the uninjured competitor?
- was the injury caused by neither competitor?

If the injury is self-inflicted, then medical aid is restricted to an examination only. If the player cannot continue, then the referee will award the contest to the uninjured player by calling '*kikengachi*' (win due to withdrawal owing to injury). The same procedure is usually followed if neither player can be blamed for the damage.

If the injury can be directly attributed to the uninjured player, then the referee will allow the injured player to receive treatment on the mat. Permitted treatment is limited to examination of the injury, movement of the limb and/or the application of a plaster. The use of sprays or ice is forbidden. In this case, should the injured player be unable to continue, then he will almost certainly be awarded the contest, with the uninjured player being disqualified.

Where a player is injured because of the actions of his opponent, but is able to continue, then, a little later, has to withdraw because of that injury, he loses the contest.

MEDICAL AID DURING A CONTEST

This rule has changed frequently throughout the history of competitive judo. Currently *no* treatment is allowed on the mat. The only exception to this is mentioned above. 'Treatment' includes the manipulation of the injured limb by the medical person. He can suggest to the player that he tries moving his arm or leg in a particular way, but he cannot move the limb himself. Nor can he use pain relief/anaesthetic sprays or ice. These are counted as 'treatment'.

In competitions involving young players in Britain, far more leeway is given on this treatment rule.

FIGURE 31 Referee signalling a call for medical attention.

Under normal circumstances, the medical aid is only brought on at the request of the referee. However, the player can ask for medical attention for minor items such as a torn fingernail or a bleeding nose. This will be indicated by the referee (see Figure 31), and on such occasions a sign is put up by the scoreboard (a red or white cross on a green background). Two such inspections are allowed. If a third is needed, the fight ends with a *kikengachi*.

If both players are injured because of an outside cause and cannot continue, the referee can call '*hikiwake*' (draw), and the contest can be refought at a later time. A refight will also be offered if both players submit simultaneously. If one player declines the refight, then the other is awarded the contest (*fusengachi*).

IOC COUNTRIES

AFG	Afghanistan	CAM	Cambodia	GEO	Georgia
AHO	Netherlands Antilles	CAN	Canada	GEQ	Equatorial Guinea
ALB	Albania	CAY	Cayman Islands	GER	Germany
ALG	Algeria	CGO	Congo	GHA	Ghana
AND	Andorra	CHA	Chad	GRE	Greece
ANG	Angora	CHI	Chile	GRN	Grenada
ANT	Antigua	CHN	China	GUA	Guatemala
ARG	Argentina	CIV	Ivory Coast	GUI	Guinea
ARM	Armenia	CMR	Cameroon	GUM	Guam
ARU	Aruba	COK	Cook Islands	GUY	Guyana
ASA	American Samoa	COL	Colombia	HAI	Haiti
AUS	Australia	COM	Comoros Islands	HKG	Hong Kong
AUT	Austria	CPV	Cape Verde	HON	Honduras
AZE	Azerbaijan	CRC	Costa Rica	HUN	Hungary
BAH	Bahamas	CRO	Croatia	INA	Indonesia
BAN	Bangladesh	CUB	Cuba	IND	India
BAR	Barbados	CYP	Cyprus	IRJ	Iran
BDI	Burundi	CZE	Czech Republic	IRL	Ireland
BEL	Belgium	DEN	Denmark	IRQ	Iraq
BEN	Benin	DJI	Djibouti	ISL	Iceland
BER	Bermuda	DMN	Dominica	ISR	Israel
BHU	Bhutan	DOM	Dominican Republic	ISV	Virgin Islands
BIH	Bosnia-Herzegovina	ECU	Ecuador	ITA	Italy
BIZ	Belize	EGY	Egypt	IVB	British Virgin Islands
BLR	Belorussia	ESA	El Salvador	JAM	Jamaica
BOL	Bolivia	ESP	Spain	JOR	Jordan
BOT	Botswana	EST	Estonia	JPN	Japan
BRA	Brazil	ETM	Ethiopia	KAZ	Kazakhstan
BRN	Bahrain	FIJ	Fiji	KEN	Kenya
BRU	Brunei	FIN	Finland	KGZ	Kyrgyzstan
BUL	Bulgaria	FRA	France	KOR	Korea (South)
BUR	Burkina Faso	GAB	Gabon	KSA	Saudi Arabia
CAF	Central African	GAM	Gambia	KUW	Kuwait
	Republic	GBR	Great Britain	LAO	Laos

LAT	Latvia	NRU	Nauru	SUI	Switzerland
LBA	Libya	NZL	New Zealand	SUR	Surinam
LBR	Liberia	OMA	Oman	SVK	Slovakia
LCA	St Lucia	PAK	Pakistan	SWE	Sweden
LES	Lesotho	PAN	Panama	SWZ	Swaziland
LIB	Lebanon	PAR	Paraguay	SYR	Syria
LIE	Lichtenstein	PER	Peru	TAN	Tanzania
LTU	Lithuania	PHI	Philippines	TGA	Tonga
LUX	Luxembourg	PLE	Palestine	THA	Thailand
MAD	Madagascar	PNG	Papua New Guinea	TJK	Tajikistan
MAR	Morocco	POL	Poland	TKM	Turkmenistan
MAS	Malaysia	POR	Portugal	TOG	Togo
MAW	Malawi	PPK	Korea (North)	TPE	Chinese Taipei
MDA	Moldavia	PUR	Puerto Rico	TRI	Trinidad and Tobago
MDV	Maldives	QAT	Qatar	TUN	Tunisia
MEX	Mexico	ROM	Romania	TUR	Turkey
MGL	Mongolia	RSA	South Africa	UAE	United Arab Emirates
MKD	Macedonia (former Yugoslav republic)	RUS	Russia	UGA	Uganda
		RWA	Rwanda	UKR	Ukraine
MLI	Mali	SAM	Western Samoa	URU	Uraguay
MLT	Malta	SEN	Senegal	USA	United States of America
MON	Monaco	SEY	Seychelles		
MOZ	Mozambique	SIN	Singapore	UZB	Uzbekistan
MRI	Mauritius	SKN	St Kitts-Nevis	VAN	Vanuatu
MTN	Mauritania	SLE	Sierra Leone	VEN	Venezuela
MYA	Myanmar (Burma)	SLO	Slovenia	VIE	Vietnam
NAM	Namibia	SMR	San Marino	VIN	St Vincent and the Grenadines
NCA	Nicaragua	SOL	Solomon Islands		
NED	Netherlands	SOM	Somalia	YEM	Yemen
NEP	Nepal	SRI	Sri Lanka	YUG	Yugoslavia
NGR	Nigeria	STP	São. Tomé and Príncipe	ZAI	Zaire
NIG	Niger			ZAM	Zambia
NOR	Norway	SUD	Sudan	ZIM	Zimbabwe

APPENDIX B

JAPANESE TERMS

In Japanese, generally, vowels are usually short and explosive sounds. The letter 'a' is pronounced as in 'hat' (except at the start of a word, when it changes to something like 'u' in 'hut'); 'e' as in 'get'; 'i' as in 'hit'; 'o' as in 'hot'; and 'u' as in 'hut' (except where I have put a macron above the letter – 'ū' – when it is pronounced like the double 'o' in 'hoot'). The Japanese words in this book are written in Romaji (Romanization) form and each letter should be pronounced. However, some letters are occasionally slurred together. For example, the first word in the list below is often pronounced as 'ak-aye'.

Japanese term	Pronunciation	Translation
akai	*ah-kah-i*	red
awasete	*ah-wah-seh-teh*	joined together
batsū	*bat-soo*	penalty
chūi	*chew-i*	(*lit.* attention) a penalty equivalent to a *yuko* score to an opponent
dojime	*doh-ji-may*	leg scissor technique
dojo	*doh-joh*	(*lit.* hall of the way) a place where judo is practised
fūsengachi	*foo-zen-gah-chi*	win by non-appearance of opponent
gachi	*gah-chi*	win
gi	*gi*	judo suit (see *judogi*)
hajime	*ha-ji-may*	begin
hansoku	*han-soh-kuh*	disqualification
hansoku gachi	*han-soh-kuh gah-chi*	win by disqualification of an opponent
hansoku make	*han-soh-kuh mah-kay*	loss by disqualification, equivalent to an *ippon* score to an opponent
hantei	*han-teh-i*	judgement or decision asked for by the referee when the scores are equal at the end of a contest
haraigoshi	*ha-ra-i-goh-shi*	sweeping hip – a judo throw
hikiwake	*hi-ki-wah-kay*	draw
ippon	*ip-pon*	one point, the ultimate score in judo
ippon shobū	*ip-pon shoh-boo*	one-point contest
jigotai	*ji-goh-tah-i*	defensive attitude or posture

Japanese term	Pronunciation	Translation
joseki	*joh-seh-ki*	place of honour in the *dojo* where guests or the most senior players sit. A player should always bow to *joseki* when he steps on to a mat as a mark of respect. If there is no physical *joseki*, it is usually accepted as being directly opposite a player when he steps on the mat
jūdogi	*joo-doh-gi*	clothing worn for judo, sometimes abbreviated to *gi*
jūdoka	*joo-doh-ka*	judo competitor(s)
jūjigatame	*joo-ji-gah-tah-may*	straight armlock
kachi	*kah-chi*	win (sometimes spelt *gachi*)
kangeiko	*can-geh-i-ko*	traditional Japanese *dojo* training week in the middle of winter
kanibasami	*can-i-bah-sah-mi*	a scissors throw
kanji	*can-ji*	Japanese writing
kansetsūwaza	*can-set-soo-wah-za*	locking techniques
katakana	*cat-a-kah-na*	Japanese writing usually used for western words and names
kawazūgake	*ka-wah-zoo-gah-kay*	an illegal action in a contest
keikokū	*keh-i-koh-koo*	(*lit.* warning) a penalty equivalent to a *waza-ari* to an opponent
kikengachi	*kick-en-gah-chi*	win owing to the retirement of an opponent during a contest, usually due to injury or illness
kinsa	*kin-za*	a minor score in judo, which does not appear on a scoreboard
kohaku shiai	*koh-ha-kuh shi-ah-i*	traditional Japanese competition
koka	*koh-ka*	(*lit.* effect) the lowest score which appears on a scoreboard
kumikata	*kuh-mi-kah-tah*	gripping, taking hold
maitta	*mah-i-ta*	'I submit'
matte	*mah-teh*	(*lit.* wait) Referee's instruction which temporarily halts the contest and brings both players back to the centre of the contest area
nagewaza	*nah-geh-wah-za*	throwing techniques
newaza	*neh-wah-za*	(*lit.* laying down techniques) ground techniques
okuriashiharai	*oh kuh-ri-ash-i-ha-rah-i*	sliding, sweeping, ankle – a judo throw
osaekomi	*oh-sah-eh-komi*	holding – referee's instruction to tell the timekeepers to start the 30-second watch for a hold-down
osaekomiwaza	*oh-sah-eh-komi-wah-za*	holding techniques
ouchigari	*oh-uh-chi-gari*	major inner reaping – a judo throw
semerū nise no	*seh-meh-roo ni-say no*	false attack
sensei	*sen-seh-i*	instructor/teacher

Japanese term	Pronunciation	Translation
seoinage	*seh-oh-i-nah-geh*	usually translated as 'shoulder throw'
shiai	*shi-ah-i*	contest
shido	*shi-doh*	(*lit.* guidance) a penalty equivalent to a *koka* to an opponent
shimewaza	*shi-meh-wa-za*	strangle technique
shinbanin	*shin-ban-in*	referee
shiroi	*shi-roh-i*	white
shochūgeiko	*shoh-chew-geh-i-ko*	traditional midsummer training week in Japanese *dojos*
sodetsūrikomigoshi	*soh-deh-t-soo-ri-komi-goh-shi*	sleeve-pulling hip – a judo throw
sogogachi	*soh-goh-gah-chi*	compound win
sonomama	*soh-noh-mah-mah*	(*lit.* as it is) referee's word to freeze the action of the players during a contest
soremade	*soh-reh-mah-deh*	(*lit.* that is all) referee's word to end a contest
sūtemiwaza	*soo-teh-mi-wah-za*	(*lit.* throw-away technique) normally translated as 'sacrifice technique'
tachiwaza	*tah-chi-wah-za*	standing technique
taisho	*tah-i-sho*	leader
tatami	*tah-tah-mi*	straw mats originally used for judo mats, nowadays applied to any judo mat
toketa	*toh-keh-ta*	referee's call to indicate that a player has escaped from a hold-down
tomoenage	*toh-moh-eh-nah-geh*	a circle throw
tori	*toh-ri*	(*lit.* the taker) the player who executes a technique
torikeshi	*toh-ri-keh-shi*	cancellation (of score)
uchimata	*uh-chi-mah-ta*	inner thigh (throw)
udegarami	*uh-deh-gah-rah-mi*	entangled armlock
uke	*uk-keh*	(*lit.* receiver) the player on whom a technique is applied
wakigatame	*wah-ki-gah-tah-meh*	armpit armlock
waza	*wah-za*	technique
waza-ari	*wah-za-a-ri*	near technique
waza-ari nichikai waza	*wah-zah-a-ri nih-chi-kah-i wah-za*	an old score equivalent to the modern score of *yuko*
yama-arashi	*yah-mah-a-rah-shi*	mountain storm – a judo throw
yoshi	*yoh-shi*	recommence fighting – referee's call following the call of 'sonomama'
yūko	*yoo-koh*	(*lit.* effect) the middle score which appears on a scoreboard
yūseigachi	*yoo-seh-i-gah-chi*	win by superiority – the expression given when a win is as a result of the decision made at *hantei* by referee and judges

INDEX

Page numbers in *italic* refer to the illustrations